Discovering
HEIRLOOM SEWING

MILNER CRAFT SERIES

Discovering HEIRLOOM SEWING

DIANA OAKLEY

SALLY MILNER PUBLISHING

First published in 1992 by
Sally Milner Publishing Pty Ltd
558 Darling Street
Rozelle NSW 2039 Australia

Reprinted in 1993

© Diana Oakley, 1992

Production by Sylvana Scannapiego,
Island Graphics
Design by Wing Ping Tong
Photography by Andre Martin
Typeset in Australia by Asset Typesetting Pty Ltd
Printed in Australia by Impact Printing

National Library of Australia
Cataloguing-in-Publication data:

Oakley, Diana.
    Discovering heirloom sewing.

    ISBN 1 86351 093 1.

    1. Machine sewing. 2. Heirlooms. I. Title.
    (Series: Milner craft series)

646.2

Dedicated to my father Ralph Clark

ACKNOWLEDGEMENTS

Thanks are due to many talented people when compiling a needlework book.

At the top of the list is Joyce Oakley, whose encouragement, friendliness and competent direction meant so much to me. Two other people deserve special mention. Carolyn Lorking kindly designed and assembled some of the patterns and samples and is responsible for the descriptive sketches and Beth Allen lovingly handstitched many of the items. I would also like to thank Jenny Haskins for her selfless enthusiasm and support as well as for providing a Pfaff 1475 CD Sewing Machine on which all the projects have been stitched. Last but by no means least, many thanks to Diana Cross for all her help.

This book would not have been possible without the love and encouragement of the special 'men' in my life.

DIANA OAKLEY 1992

CONTENTS

HEIRLOOM SEWING

French handsewing by machine, heirloom sewing and heritage sewing are just a few of the names given to an age-old craft. French handsewing has been popular for many years, but in the late 1970s, some Southern women in the United States decided to devise a quicker method for achieving the same results. What they came up with involved using the zig zag on their sewing machines — and the technique only took a fraction of the time of the original.

As is often the case with innovations, other ideas evolved as a result of their discovery. There are various ways of doing heirloom sewing by machine, but I have found that the techniques used in this book are the strongest, fastest and simplest.

The techniques, terms, fabrics and trimmings are the same as those used in French handsewing. One of the joys of heirloom sewing is being able to join laces, fabric and embroideries to create your own fabric.

Before beginning to sew a project, you should experiment with each of the techniques and find the correct settings for your machine. You may like to keep a 'recipe' card and write down all the settings for each technique. This will save time when next you sit down to sew.

The aim of this book is to teach you the techniques of heirloom sewing. I hope you will enjoy this craft as much as I do.

 GLOSSARY

LACE TERMS

Baby Lace   A narrow lace edging or insertion.

Beading   A lace or embroidered insertion, edging or galloon (narrow, close-woven braid) with small holes through which a ribbon is laced.

Binche Lace   A very fine, cotton, straight-edged lace characterised by a spotted design. Originally handmade in Flanders; machine-made reproductions are produced in England, France and the United States.

Bobbin Lace   General term describing handmade lace made with bobbins on special lace-making pillows or bolsters. Following a pricked pattern, pins are inserted in the lace while it is being made to keep all the thread crossings in place until that portion is secure. Handmade Valenciennes, Binche, Mechin, Chantilly and Honiton are some examples of bobbin lace.

Cluny Lace   A heavy cotton lace with a geometric design, often featuring radiating wheat ears.

Cordonnet   A distinctive, heavier thread that outlines the design in a lace. Cordonnet can also refer to a type of needlework thread as in DMC's Cordonnet Special.

Filet Lace   A lace worked with a needle, comprising square meshes partially filled to create a design. Also the name given to crochet lace of similar design.

Irish Crocheted   A cotton lace made by crocheting to form characteristic designs of layered rose petals and shamrocks with picoted brides (bars).

Malines   An open-textured, diamond-shaped mesh.

Mechlin   A bobbin-lace mesh of very fine thread. Early Mechlin lace had a six-sided mesh ground. However, present-day Mechlin lace is often found with a diamond-shaped ground. It is usually characterised by floral motifs with a fine Cordonnet. It is lighter in weight than Alencon, not as strong as Valenciennes.

Limerick Lace   A delicate handmade lace worked by embroidering a variety of stitches onto a fine cotton net. This lace is ideal for collars, cuffs and medallions. May also be French hand or machine sewn.

Picot Lace   An edging with narrow, triangular or rounded loops along the outside edge.

Tatting   A type of lace made by looping and knotting a thread that is wound on a hand shuttle.

Valenciennes Lace (Val)   A fine, cotton, bobbin lace, usually with a hexagonal or diamond-shaped mesh background. Originally made by hand and later by machine in Valenciennes, France. Most widely used lace in fine hand or machine sewing.

Vraile   French for real or handmade.

STITCHES

Broderie Anglaise   A form of white embroidery characterised by eyelet holes surrounded by buttonhole stitches.

Bullion Knot   Similar to a French knot but covering a length of stitches formed by wrapping the thread around the needle and passing the needle through the cloth to anchor it.

Faggoting   A decorative buttonhole-type stitch to join two finished edges. Faggoting involves embroidering over the space between the two. The stitching may be either plain or knotted.

Feather Stitch   A tiny, decorative, surface embroidery loosely resembling a vine, often found on infants' garments. May also be worked as double or triple feather stitch.

French Knot A small knot formed by wrapping the thread around the point of the needle to make a knot on the surface of fabric. The thread is then carried back to the wrong side.

French Laid Work Embroidery characterised by use of padded, raised satin-stitch motifs. Used at the turn of the century to embellish French handsewn garments. It was often combined with Broderie anglaise and other white-work embroidery stitches for textural contrasts.

Hemstitch A decorative stitch made by drawing out threads running parallel to the hem and fastening the cross threads with stitches, leaving an openwork effect. May be used as an insertion or hem finish; variations include half, ladder and serpentine hemstitch.

Lazy Daisy Also known as the detached chain stitch. Lazy daisy stitches, when grouped, form flowers or leaves in embroidery designs.

Point de Paris (Pin Stitch) A decorative stitch characterised by tiny pierced holes, used to apply edging, curved Madeira appliqué, to finish a flat-felled seam and as a decorative method of sewing a hem.

Satin Stitch A straight stitch solidly covering a given motif.

Shadow Work Embroidery worked on a transparent fabric so that the threads on the back show through, producing delicate shadow effect. It may be worked from the right side using double back stitch, or from the wrong side using closed herringbone.

Shell Stitch A decorative, scalloped stitch formed by folding a narrow hem and working a blanket stitch at intervals over the folded edge.

SEWING TERMS

Butterfly Sleeve A sleeve cut in half vertically from shoulder to sleeve hem and jointed at the hem. May have lace edging along rolled and whipped cut edges.

Crosswise Grain The threads across a woven fabric that run from selvedge to selvedge; also called the filling, woof or weft yarns.

French Seam A self-enclosed seam formed by stitching wrong sides together, trimmed to 3 mm (⅛″) width, and stitching a second time with right sides together. Usually used on lightweight fabrics where cut edges would fray.

Growth Tucks Tucks placed in dress during construction and let out later to accommodate growing children.

Hem Edge of material folded over and, usually, sewn to protect a raw finish.

Lengthwise Grain Refers to threads that run parallel to the selvedge in a woven fabric; also known as the warp yarns.

Mitre The diagonal joining of two edges at a corner.

Placket An opening at the neck, on sleeve cuffs or in the skirt of a garment.

Selvedge The tightly woven edge down each side of a fabric. The word means 'self-edge' (ie. its own edge).

Slip Stitch A tiny, durable stitch suitable for a folded hem edge; the stitches are slipped through the fold of the hem edge.

Thread Loops Tiny fastening for buttons created by:
1. working a buttonhole stitch over anchored threads, or
2. crocheting with a fine crochet hook and sewing thread, or
3. tatting thread loops.

True Bias A 45° angle to any straight edge when fabric grains are perpendicular.

Tucks Stitched folds of fabric used for decoration or shaping.
1. Pintuck — Tuck with a very narrow space between the stitching line and the fold line.
2. Released tuck — Tuck generally used to create fullness, going only part of the way down a garment.

3. Shell tuck — A decorative tuck secured by stitching the shell stitch over the folded edge.

4. Spaced tucks — Tucks with spaces between them.

5. Whipped tuck — Tuck which is created by whipping a tiny slant stitch over a folded edge of fabric, encompassing only two or three threads. Generally used to create a feeling of texture. Whipped tucks can also be curved and be made on the bias.

FABRICS

Batiste   A sheer, fine-woven fabric with a plain weave. Made of cotton, cotton blends, wool, silk, rayon or other fibres.

Cambric   A soft, white, closely woven cotton fabric calendered (pressed by rollers in a machine) to give a lustre on the right side. Originally made in Cambrai, France, of linen.

Challis   One of the softest fabrics made, usually with a plain weave. Originally made of wool, but now of cotton, rayon or a wide variety of blends.

Dimity   From the Greek word meaning 'double thread'. Dimity is a lightweight, woven cotton fabric (similar to lawn). It is made by weaving two or more yarns as one and separating them with areas of plain weave, giving a checked or barred effect.

Dotted Swiss   A lightweight cotton or cotton-blend fabric woven from fine yarns and embellished with woven or flocked small dots.

Handkerchief Linen   A lightweight fabric with a plain weave. Made from the flax plant. Handkerchief linen is similar in lustre to batiste but the yarns are more uneven than cotton yarns.

Lawn   A lightweight cotton fabric with a plain weave. Crisper than batiste but not as crisp as organdy.

Nainsook   A soft-finished cotton fabric similar to batiste but less transparent. Slightly heavier and coarser than lawn.

Organza   A very light, sheer, stiff fabric similar to organdy but made of silk or man-made fibres.

Organdy (Organdie)   A very light, sheer, cotton fabric with a plain weave and a finish that gives it a characteristic crispness.

Ramie   A fabric of natural fibre — made from a nettle plant. Similar in character to handkerchief linen. Ramie has more lustre than linen and can be woven into fabric as fine as imported Swiss batiste.

Swiss Batiste   A sheer, transparent fabric with a high lustre. It has a special finish and is made using special grades of longstaple cotton and Swiss mercerisation.

THE FINEST TRIMMINGS IN THE WORLD

Swiss embroideries and French Val laces are known the world over to be among the finest trimmings ever produced. They are like the Rolls Royce — no others compare.

Both the Swiss and the French use the finest cottons available for their products. When you compare Swiss embroideries to others, you will easily observe that the Swiss white is the brightest of whites. To the touch, you will sense a superior choice of fabric — the famous cotton Swiss batiste.

One characteristic of the French Val laces that cannot be copied is evident in the gathering threads. These unique, delicate threads run along the top of a lace edge or on both sides of a lace insertion. They allow the lace to be shaped or gathered without the need for additional thread which would bulk or distort the delicate lace design.

Patterns produced on the very old French Leaver lace machines and the modern Swiss Schifli embroidery machines are those most copied by other producers of trimmings. However, these copies are not made with cotton of the same high quality; in fact, cotton blends or nylons are usually used, and the results are quite disappointing in comparison.

Factors such as different gray goods (undyed woven or knitted fabrics) and not setting machinery to produce the same number of stitches per centimetre as the Swiss, clearly result in embroidery designs that have less appeal to the purists. Fortunately, the Swiss still choose to use these extra stitches; this may slow the machinery down and add to the cost, but it results in a cleaner, more distinctive pattern. However, other trimmings that cost much less to produce are ideal for craft and sewing projects not intended to become treasured, priceless heirlooms.

French handsewers, English smockers and, today, those of us who do heirloom sewing on the sewing machine still demand the finest in sewing products. Tradition has dictated that we continue to use French Val laces, Swiss embroideries, Swiss batiste and Swiss organdy of the same quality as those used on our beloved family heirlooms. We are stitching new heirlooms, and in order for them to be preserved in the best possible condition and stand the test of time, the natural fibres found in traditional trimmings and fabrics are essential.

SWISS EMBROIDERIES

ENTREDEUX

This piece of trimming is designed to add strength to any part of a garment or project that will receive a lot of stress or pull. Entredeux is a French word meaning 'between the two'. Many of the sewing machines today can create a stitch similar to Swiss entredeux. However, domestic sewing machines will never be able to produce as many stitches per centimetre as the Swiss embroidery machines. Therefore, the Swiss-made entredeux is the one to use for heirloom sewing where there is to be stress or pull.

DOUBLE ENTREDEUX

This may be used in the same manner as the single entredeux.

TRIPLE ENTREDEUX

Has the same uses as the other entredeux.

TWO-TRACK ENTREDEUX

This piece of trimming is excellent for machine or hand embroidery.

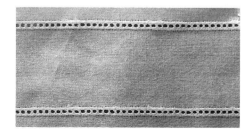

ENTREDEUX BEADING

Has the same uses as the entredeux, but may also be used for threading ribbon.

INSERTION

These insertions also come in colours. They must be rolled and whipped before use.

INSERTION

These insertions with the entredeux attached are very useful because they save one step in having to attach the entredeux.

BEADING INSERTION

As with the Swiss insertion, one step is saved in joining. This one has the holes for threading the ribbon.

NARROW EDGING

As the name implies, this trimming is used as an edging, eg, for neck, sleeves or hem.

WIDE EDGING

These wider trimmings are used for pleating in smocking and as an edging.

GALLOON

A galloon is an insertion with a scallop on each side.

GALLOON BEADING

This variation features holes for ribbon insertion.

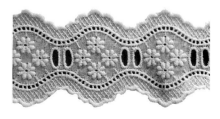

SWISS EMBROIDERY FAMILY

FRENCH VAL LACES

BEADING

Used as an insertion for threading ribbon.

GALLOON BEADING

Also used as an insertion for threading ribbon, but features a scallop on each side.

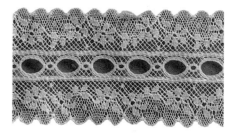

INSERTION

As the name suggests, this trimming is used for insertion between fabrics or other trimmings. Note the heading on either side (in a heavier thread) which has three or four threads running along. These are used for shaping.

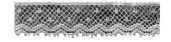

NARROW EDGING

Used for trimming neck edges, sleeves, hem lines, etc. Note the gathering threads in the heading.

WIDE EDGING

Used for trimming sleeves and hem lines, etc. Also features the gathering threads.

FRENCH VAL LACE FAMILY

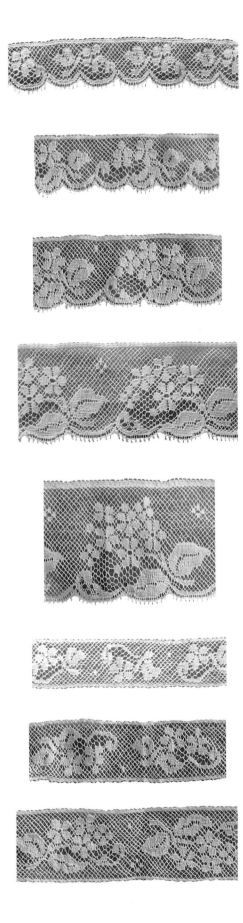

# MATERIALS

FABRICS

There are numerous fabrics suitable for heirloom sewing. I prefer pure fabrics, but there are many blends which can be used.

Suggestions: Batiste, voile, lawn, Liberty prints, linen, organdy, wool challis, velvet and tartans.

THREADS

DMC 50 or Madeira Tanne 80 is recommended. These are 100% cotton and very fine. A much better result is achieved with fine threads because the stitches are not as visible. When stitching on coloured fabrics, use the thread to match the fabric. However, when attaching the trimmings, use the thread to match the trimmings. If doing twin needlework, always purchase two reels of thread.

NEEDLES

The finest needles available for your machine should be used, about 70. Always start a project with a new needle.

Twin Needles: Once again, fine needles are needed. When pintucking, twin needles should be tested with your pintucking foot to make sure you have the appropriate needles for the appropriate foot. Place the twin needles in the grooves of the pintucking foot; if the needles splay or spread apart, you will know to change either the foot or the needles.

TRIMMINGS

It is unnecessary to preshrink French Val laces and Swiss embroideries. This has been done during their manufacture. However, I do recommend using a spray starch and steam pressing each piece before commencing. This will make them easier to handle.

Baby's Shawl (Project 9) and Baby's Pillow (Project 2)

Detail of Baby's Pillow

Pillow (Project 1)

Lace Collar (Project 3)

Detail of Lace Collar

Detail of Nightie Bodice

Nightie (Project 4)

Baby's Basket Set (Project 5)

Detail of Bag and Pin Cushion from Baby's Basket Set

Collar (Project 6)

Detail of Collar

Train Suit (Project 7)

Detail of Train Suit

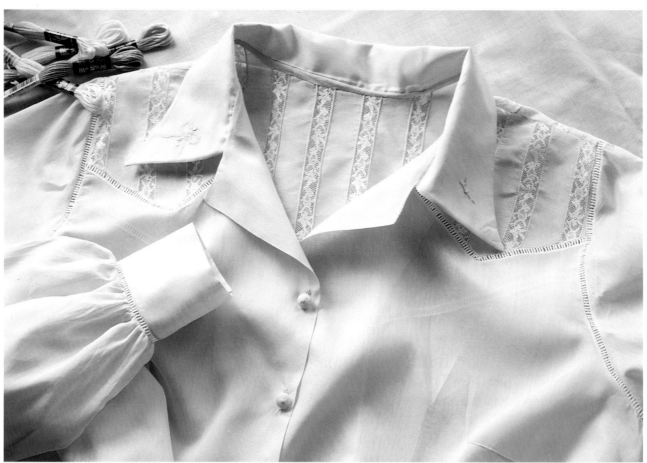

Blouse (Project 8)

Back of Blouse

TECHNIQUES

ROLL AND WHIP

This is the most important of techniques; on it rests the success or failure of your project. There must always be a firm base on which to attach your trimmings — if you were to attach trimmings directly onto a raw edge, they would easily pull away. A rolled and whipped edge provides the firm base that is required.

Set your machine to a zig zag stitch. The settings will need to be adjusted so the needle will zig on the fabric no more than 3 mm (⅛″), then zag off the raw edge completely.

Now that your setting for rolling and whipping is set, you are ready to start. As the needle zigs and zags backwards and forwards you will see how the edge of the fabric is rolling it doesn't matter whether it rolls over or under, or both, as this will not show once you add your next piece (Fig. 1).

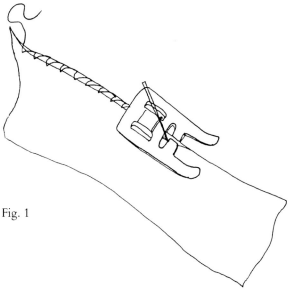

Fig. 1

ROLL, WHIP AND GATHER

This is a very useful technique for gathering fabric for waistbands and sleeves, and for frills and puffing (Fig. 3). The same technique as for rolling and whipping will be used, except that a gathering thread will be added at the same time. You will have to check with your machine dealer to find out which foot is the best one to use for this technique — each machine is different. Some have a small hole in the foot or a groove underneath, through which a fine cord or thicker thread can be inserted.

I use DMC Perle 8 or 12 for this technique, but there are others, such as a quilting thread, that are suitable, as long as they are strong enough not to

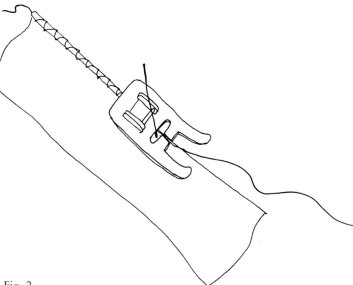

Fig. 2

26

break when pulled up for gathering. The setting on your machine will be the same as for rolling and whipping. Place your gathering thread under your presser foot and on top of the fabric, close to the raw edge. Zig zag over the thread using the same technique as before. The zig zag will roll the edge, encasing the thread (Fig. 2).

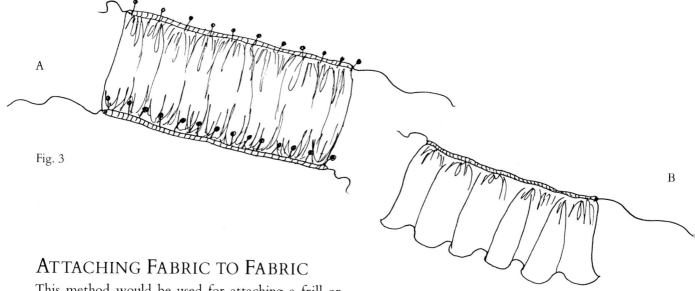

A

Fig. 3

B

ATTACHING FABRIC TO FABRIC

This method would be used for attaching a frill or puffing strip where no entredeux is used. Using the same setting as for rolling and whipping, place the two rolled and whipped edges, right sides together, one edge just inside the other. Zig over these two edges and zag off the rolled edge to the right (Fig 4).

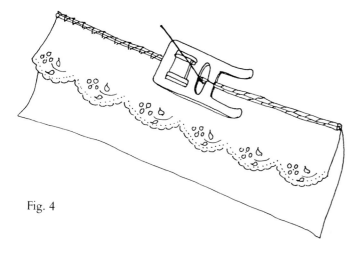

Fig. 4

ATTACHING ENTREDEUX TO FABRIC

Take a piece of entredeux and check the stitch length. Place the entredeux under the presser foot and, still using the zig zag setting, adjust the stitch length so that the needle goes into each entredeux hole once; the width should be the same as before.

Now that the setting is correct, note it in your book ready for next time. Take the piece of entreduex you wish to attach to the fabric, and cut away the batiste from *one* edge only. Place the entredeux with right sides together, just inside the rolled and whipped edge, not on top of it. If it is placed on top, it will roll off as it goes under the presser foot. I always work with the entredeux on the left-hand side at all times, I find this a lot easier (also, old habits die hard). Put the needle down into the entredeux hole, then put the presser foot down, zag off the fabric (Fig. 5) and then zig back into the next hole.

When attaching entredeux to gathered fabric the same rules apply.

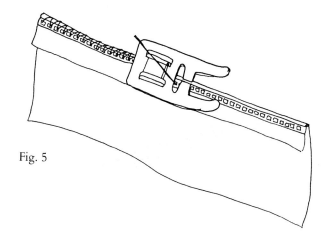

Fig. 5

ATTACHING LACE TO FABRIC

In most cases, the required setting on your machine will be the same as for rolling and whipping, depending on the width of the lace heading. In this instance, the fabric has already been rolled and whipped. Place the lace, right sides together, just inside the rolled and whipped edge as before. Then, checking that the needle will zig zag over the heading of the lace and zag off the edge to the right, attach the lace (Fig. 6). It is important that this heading is covered. If not, the lace can change shape because this is where the gathering threads are located.

When attaching gathered lace to fabric, gather your lace by pulling the threads in the heading. I always like to take one thread from the top of the heading and one from the bottom; this way the heading will stay flat when it is attached to the fabric.

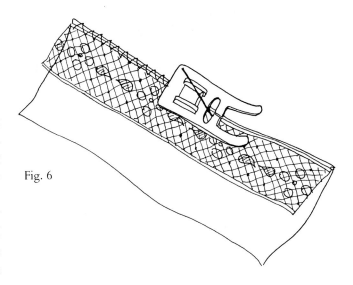

Fig. 6

PROJECT 1 – PILLOW

PILLOW

This project has been prepared to give you some practice in the techniques just described.

MATERIALS

Fabric: Swiss batiste 112 cm wide x 20 cm (45″ x 8″)

Swiss insertion (without entredeux): 65734 x 20 cm (8″)

Wide Swiss edging: 65735 x 1.50 m (5 ft)

Entredeux beading: 59183 x 40 cm (16″)

Lace insertion: 2033 x 40 cm (16″)

INSTRUCTIONS

1. Cut three pieces of batiste 20 cm x 26 cm (8″ x 10½″). Two of these will be for making the insert for the pillow.

2. Take one piece and roll and whip all edges, using the Roll and Whip technique.

3. Cut four strips 20 cm x 4 cm (8″ x 1¾″). Roll and whip all edges.

4. Roll and whip all edges of the Swiss insertion.

5. Cut entredeux beading in half and attach to both sides of the Swiss insertion, using the Entredeux to Fabric technique.

6. To the other side of both pieces of entredeux beading, attach one of the fabric strips, using the same method.

7. Cut the lace insertion in half and attach to the fabric strips, using the technique of Lace to Fabric.

8. Attach the other two pieces of fabric to the lace strips.

9. Thread ribbon through the entredeux beading, completing the construction of your 'fabric'.

10. Using the Roll, Whip and Gather technique, take the Swiss edging and roll, whip and gather.

11. Measure around the piece of fabric you have made and draw up the edging to this length.

12. With right sides together and using the same setting as for roll and whip, attach the edging to the fabric piece you have made, being sure to allow fullness on the corners.

13. Take one of the 20 cm x 26 cm (8″ x 10½″) pieces of batiste. Place with right sides together and attach in the same way as you did the edging, leaving an opening for the insert cushion.

14. Make up the insert cushion and fill with the desired amount of filling.

15. Place inside pillow and neatly handstitch the opening together.

ECHNIQUES

ENTREDEUX TO LACE

If you are using the same size of entredeux as you did for the previous project, the stitch length required should be the same for this technique. Cut the batiste away from one side of your entredeux. Place the lace and the entredeux side by side, with the entredeux on the left. As the needle zags to the right, make sure it goes over the heading on the lace, then back into the next entredeux hole (Fig. 7A). If you keep the entredeux and the lace very slightly apart (Fig. 7B) the stitch will draw them neatly together as they go under the presser foot. If you butt them side by side, they are pulled on top of one another as they go under the presser foot, and you do not get such a neat finish.

When attaching entredeux to gathered lace, the same technique is used.

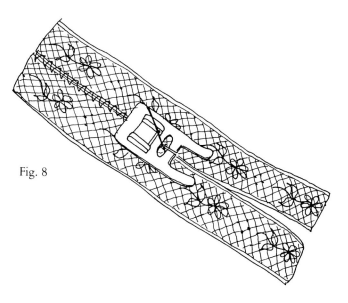
Fig. 7

LACE TO LACE

Using the same technique as Entredeux to Lace, butt the laces together, zig onto the left, making sure to cover the heading, and zag to the right, making sure to cover the heading (Fig. 8). As with Entredeux to Lace, keep the laces slightly apart as they go under the presser foot.

When applying Gathered Lace to Lace, the same technique is used.

Fig. 8

JOINING LACE

When joining two ends of lace together, a better result is achieved if the pattern can be matched. Having decided on which pattern, place them on top of one another. Using a fine zig zag stitch, follow the pattern carefully, stitching around the edge of the flower or design (Fig. 9). After stitching, cut away carefully, following the stitching line (Fig. 10).

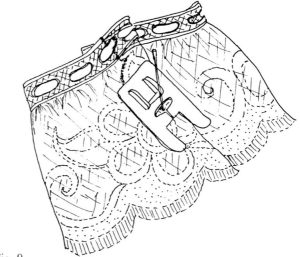

Fig. 9

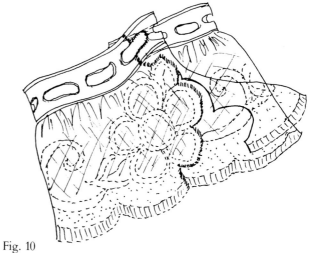

Fig. 10

PROJECT 2 – BABY'S PILLOW

BABY'S PILLOW

MATERIALS

Fabric: Wool Challis 152 cm wide x 30 cm
  (60" x 12")
Entredeux beading: 61925 x 1.20 m (48")
Lace insertion: E7911 1/2 x 1.80 m (72")
Lace edging: E7913 x 3.10 m (124")

INSTRUCTIONS

1. Cut one strip of fabric 6 cm x 45 cm (2½" x 18").

2. Using the Roll, Whip and Gather technique, stitch both sides of this piece.

3. Gather it up evenly, on both sides to 30 cm (12") in length. This is called 'puffing'.

4. Pin this piece on the ironing board, then steam with an iron held above, not on, the puffing. Leave to dry.

5. While the puffing strip is drying, join the lace insertions, using the Lace to Lace technique. Cut six strips 30 cm (12") long. Watching carefully to ensure the patterns on the lace match, join three strips together, and then the other three strips together (two separate lots).

6. Cut two strips of fabric 30 cm x 7 cm (12" x 3"). Roll and whip edges.

7. To one side only of these two strips, add entredeux beading, using the Entredeux to Fabric technique. Also add the entredeux beading to both sides of the puffing strip.

8. Taking the puffing strip with entredeux beading attached, join the two lots of laces, one set on each side.

9. Now join the laces to the other strips of fabric that have the entredeux beading attached.

10. Thread ribbon through beading. Make a bow and attach if desired.

11. Roll and whip around all unfinished edges.

12. Gather the edging lace and measure carefully, adjusting gatherings for corners. When you have the desired length, join the lace together so you have a circle, using the Joining Lace technique. Attach right around edge using the Lace to Fabric technique.

13. For the back of the pillow, attach a piece of fabric 40 cm x 30 cm (16″ x 12″) that has been rolled and whipped, as in Project 1.

14. Make inner cushion. Insert and finish as in Project 1.

ECHNIQUES

ROLL AND WHIP CURVED OR BIAS EDGE

This technique is applied to armholes, neck edges or round yokes. First, stay stitch 3 mm (⅛″) from the raw edge. Trim as close to that stitching as you can (Fig. 11). Now, using the Roll and Whip technique, stitch over the stay stitching (Fig. 12).

This same technique can be used when gathering the top of a sleeve, only we prefer the Roll, Whip and Gather technique.

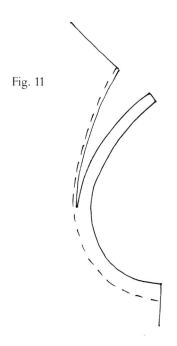

Fig. 11

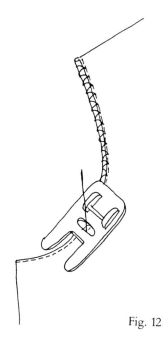

Fig. 12

ENTREDEUX TO CURVED EDGE

This technique is used for neck edges, armholes and round yokes, or when making different shapes such as ovals, circles, hearts, etc.

Make a pattern of the shape to which you wish to attach the entredeux. Place the pattern on a soft surface, where you can pin (I always use the ironing board). Cut the batiste from one edge of the entredeux and start pinning it around the pattern, clipping the other batiste edge as you go (Fig. 13). Spray starch and steam press. Leave to dry for a few minutes.

Now take the shaped entredeux, butting it to the rolled and whipped edge of fabric. Then attach by zigging into each entredeux hole once and zagging over the rolled and whipped edge (Fig. 14).

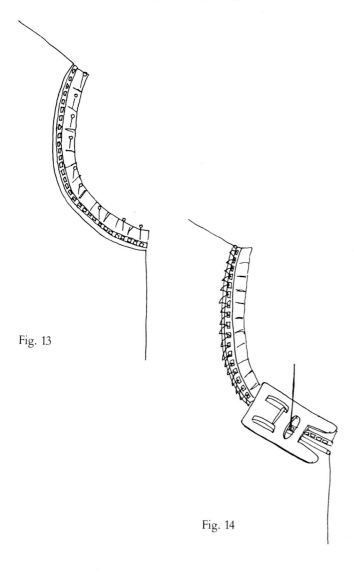

Fig. 13

Fig. 14

ENTREDEUX TO CORNER

Measure your entredeux so it is about four or five holes longer than needed. Attach this piece, leaving the extra holes unattached (Fig. 15). Attach the piece coming the other way and overlap the holes (Fig. 16).

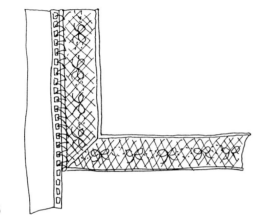

Fig. 15

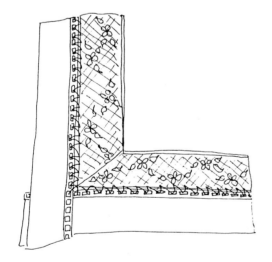

Fig. 16

LACE EDGING TO CURVED EDGE

It is important to know if you wish the lace to stand up or lie flat before commencing. If the lace is to stand up, then the lace is butted to the rolled and whipped edge of the fabric (Fig. 17). The lace must be gathered first. If you wish the lace to lie down, place it right sides together with the fabric (Fig. 18).

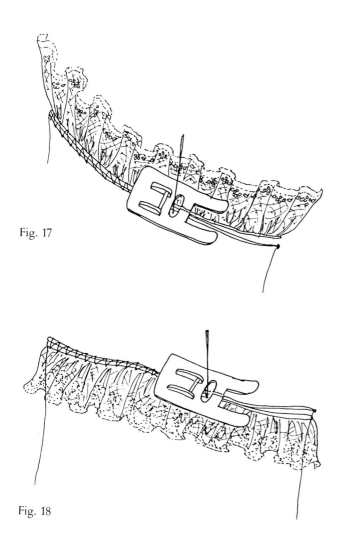

Fig. 17

Fig. 18

PROJECT 3 – LACE COLLAR

LACE COLLAR

Take any bodice pattern with a high, round neck. Determine the length of your collar. The one I have made is 30 cm (12″) from the shoulder, before adding edging lace.

I have given the quantities used in this collar, but you may have to alter them slightly, depending on the size you require. You will be making two rectangles of 'fabric' the required length and the width of the bodice pattern. This one measures 30 cm in length and 42 cm wide (12″ x 17″).

Hint: When 'making fabric' with lace as in this project, I have found it very helpful, after you have joined a couple of pieces, to put a thread on the right side at the top. Then, each time you have to add a piece of lace, you don't have to examine closely to see which is the right or wrong side. This speeds the project considerably.

MATERIALS
Narrow lace insertion: 837 x 13.2 m (14½ yd)
Wide lace insertion: 839 x 4.2 m (4⅔ yd)
Entredeux: 30054 x 11 m (12 yd)
Narrow lace edging: 831 x 60 cm (24″)
Wide lace edging: 832 x 3.4 m (3¾ yd)

INSTRUCTIONS

1. Take the wider insertion and cut a strip the desired length.

2. Cut two pieces of entredeux the same length. Attach, using the Entredeux to Lace technique.

3. Cut six strips of narrow insertion, being careful to match the patterns or have them alternating. Join two of these pieces one each side of the entredeux, using the Entredeux to Lace technique.

4. Join the other pieces (two each side) to the lace strips you have just added, using Lace to Lace technique.

5. Now add two more strips of entredeux, one each side, to these lace strips.

6. You should now have one wide insertion, with entredeux each side. On each side of that there will be three strips of narrow insertions, then a strip of entredeux on each side of that.

7. Continue to join laces and entredeux in this manner until the required width is reached (wide insertion, entredeux, narrow insertions by three, entredeux, wide insertion, entredeux, narrow insertions by three, etc.)

8. Now that you have two rectangles of 'fabric', place these on your pattern and trace around the shape of the neck and shoulders (Fig. 19). Cut this out, noting that the back piece will have a higher neckline than the front.

9. Stay stitch the necklines.

10. Join the right shoulders with a French seam.

11. Roll and whip lower edges.

12. Attach entredeux, using the Entredeux to Lace technique, starting at the open seam. When reaching a corner, use the Entredeux to Corner technique. Attach entredeux all around the edge, leaving the neck edge for the moment.

13. Gather the wide edging lace, attach around edge, using Entredeux to Gather Lace technique, making sure there is sufficient fullness on the corners.

14. Roll and whip neck edge. Attach entredeux using Entredeux to Curved Edge technique. Gather and attach the narrow edging, using the Lace Edging to Curved Edge technique.

15. Make a fine hem on each left shoulder seam. Attach clear press studs and antique lace buttons.

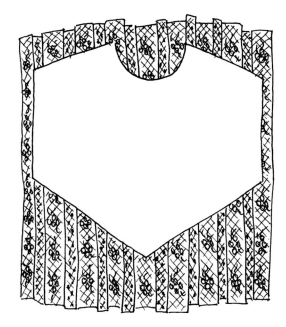

Fig. 19

ROJECT 4 – NIGHTIE

NIGHTIE

MATERIALS

Fabric: Swiss batiste 112 cm wide x 1.50 m (45″ x 1⅔ yd)

Lace insertion: 1902 x 12 m (13 yd)

Swiss insertion with Entredeux: 67143/A x 15 m (16¼ yd)

Swiss edging: 67143 x 7 m (7¾ yd)

Entredeux beading: 59183 x 1.20 m (1⅓ yd)

Ribbon: 3 mm (⅛″) x 2.3 m (2½ yd)

INSTRUCTIONS

1. Take bodice pattern and measure length from shoulder. Allow an extra 1 cm (½″) and cut lace and Swiss insertions this length, being careful to match patterns.

2. Join these pieces alternately — lace insertion, Swiss insertion — using the Entredeux to Lace technique. Make two pieces, front and back.

3. When the desired width is reached, place the pattern on this 'fabric piece' and cut out. Remember not to throw the leftovers away as these can be used for other projects.

4. Join with French seam at the shoulders.

5. Roll and whip around all raw edges.

6. Add entredeux to the neckline, using the Entredeux to Corner technique.

7. Measure around the neckline and allow 1½ times the length for the Swiss edging.

8. Using the Roll, Whip and Gather technique, gather this edging. Join to the entredeux, using the Entredeux to Lace (gathered) technique. I chose to gather at the corners rather than mitre as I felt it gave a softer look. When joining the Swiss edging, join at a shoulder seam with a French seam.

9. Roll, whip and gather the Swiss edging for the armholes, using the same technique; attach.

10. Attach entredeux beading to the bottom of the bodice, using Entredeux to Fabric technique.

11. Halve the length of fabric purchased and use a full width for the skirt. Join the side seams with a French seam.

12. Using the Roll, Whip and Gather technique, gather one end of skirt.

13. Attach this to the bodice using Entredeux to Fabric (gathered) technique.

14. Roll and whip lower edge of skirt.

15. Attach Swiss insertion, lace insertion, Swiss insertion alternately.

16. Roll, whip and gather the Swiss edging and attach to Swiss insertion. Note there is only one seam with edging and insertions.

17. Thread ribbon through the endredeux beading. Attach a small bow at the neckline, if desired.

Place on fold

Pattern for Nightie Bodice

43

ECHNIQUES

TWIN NEEDLE PINTUCKS

This is an advanced technique and may not be done easily on all sewing machines.

You will need a twin needle; I prefer 1.6/70. Earlier in the section on Needles, I explained how to match the right needle with the right pintucking foot. Make sure you do this. Speak with your machine dealer to find out how to thread your machine for this technique; each machine has its own idiosyncrasies. Also, check how to thread a cord for pintucking.

Cut and straighten a piece of fabric at least 5 cm (2″) wider than the finished piece you wish to pintuck. This will vary depending on the number of rows you wish to pintuck and the size of cord you wish to use. I prefer not to use anything heavier than DMC Perle 8. The length should be at least 5 cm (2″) longer than you will need.

Spray starch and steam press the fabric. Fold the fabric in half, length to length, make a seam and press seam to one side. This will give you a tube (Fig. 20). Place the fabric around the free arm of your machine. Line up the edge of the fabric with a mark on your machine in order to keep the first pintuck straight. As you arrive back at the beginning of that first pintuck, move the fabric across so that the first pintuck is in the next or second groove. Keeping it there, complete that row (Fig. 21). Continue in this manner until desired number of pintucks have been worked.

When you have finished tucking, cut through the tube at the seam.

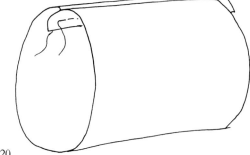

Fig. 20

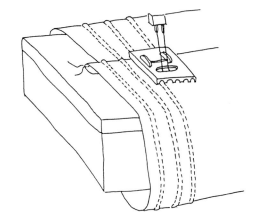

Fig. 21

PROJECT 5 – BABY'S BASKET SET

Baby's Basket Set

MATERIALS

These are the Swiss embroideries used in this project.

Insertion: 68360 Champagne
Beading: 68359 Champagne
Narrow edging: 68361 Champagne
Wide edging: 68362/A Champagne

Basket

The basket I have used for this project was my baby basket many moons ago. It would be pointless for me to give you the measurements for this as they would not apply to your needs. First, find your own basket!

To make a pattern of the base, sit the basket on a piece of paper and draw around it. As you have used the outside measurement this will include a seam allowance. Cut a piece of fabric the size of your pattern. This could be quilted, if you wish.

Measure around the sides of the basket and double the measurement. The width of this strip will be the depth of the sides plus sufficient to fold over the top about 2.5 cm (1″). Roll, whip and gather both long edges, after joining into a circle. One edge will be gathered into the base; the other edge will be attached to a Swiss beading. Attach the beading to a wide Swiss edging. Thread ribbon through the beading and draw up to fit the basket.

Cotton Wool Bag

If you have some scraps left over from the Lace Collar or the Nightie bodice, you can make a piece of 'fabric' 15 cm x 30 cm (6" x 12"). This will then be sufficient to make the bag and the pin cushion. Otherwise, make a piece of 'fabric' with the insertions and pintucking to the required measurement.

1. Cut the piece of 'fabric' 16 cm (6½") long, and a piece of plain fabric for the back.

2. Join these two pieces together with a French seam. Roll and whip the top edge.

3. Attach a beading, and then a narrow edging to the beading.

4. Thread ribbon through and embroider, if desired.

Pin Cushion

This can be made any shape you like. We made ours in an oval, 14 cm x 10 cm (5½" x 4").

1. Cut this size from the 'fabric' made when working the Cotton Wool Bag.

2. Roll and whip all around the edge. Measure around oval and cut narrow edging 1½ times this length.

3. Roll, whip and gather this edging. With right sides together, attach to oval.

4. Cut a piece of plain fabric for the back. Roll and whip edge. With right sides together and leaving an opening for turning, attach to front piece.

5. Turn and press. Fill with wadding and finish opening neatly by hand. Embroidery may be stitched if desired, before joining.

A powder tin and tissue box are also suitable items for covering.

TECHNIQUES

FOLDING LACE

Lace can also be folded into a shape, eg. a bow. This is done on top of the fabric. Start by drawing a shape as in Fig. 22. Following this shape, fold the lace (Fig. 23), until your bow shape has been completed (Fig. 24). Tack in position. Now zig zag over the heading on the lace, through the fabric, around the outside edge. Then zig zag on the inside edge. Very carefully cut the fabric away from the back.

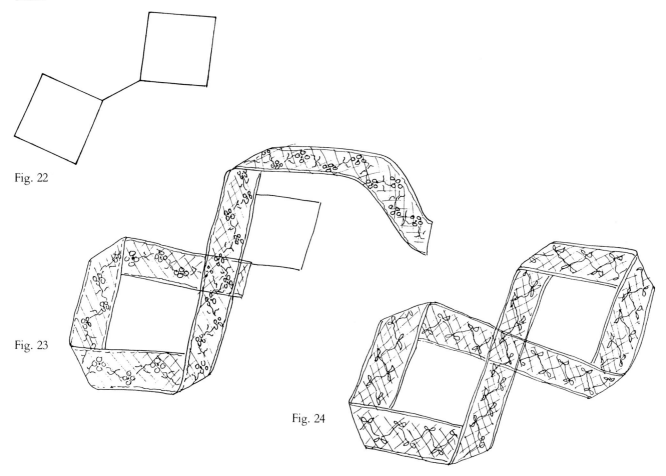

Fig. 22

Fig. 23

Fig. 24

 # PROJECT 6 – COLLAR

COLLAR

MATERIALS
Fabric: 30 cm (12″)
Insertion: 1.3 m (1½ yd)
Edging: 3 m (3⅓ yd)

INSTRUCTIONS

1. Cut out the top and sides of the collar, leaving the bottom edge straight.

2. Attach back and front shoulder seams with a very narrow French seam.

3. With the front of the collar facing you and right side up, pintuck left edge, starting ½-1 cm (¼-½″) from edge and using ½ cm (¼″) pintucks. Do 16 for the small collar, 18 for the medium and 20 for the large.

4. Lay and pin the insertion lace ½ cm (¼″) in from the last pintuck, taking it up the front, over the shoulder and down the back, as shown on the pattern. Ease the lace in with the gathering thread in the heading of the lace, over the shoulder until it fits.

5. Attach lace along heading with a straight stitch first, then go over stitching with a zig zag stitch wide enough to cover all of the heading.

6. Place a small piece of insertion lace diagonally on the collar as shown on pattern and attach as above.

7. Pin insertion lace into a bow as shown on collar pattern, making sure to cover the join of the two insertion laces. Attach as for other insertion.

8. Find centre front of collar and cut out bottom edge. Then cut out bottom edge of back and check to make sure lace edge fits. Adjust back width so lace fits edge to edge at neckline. Do not overlap.

9. Roll and whip right around the collar. Attach gathered lace edge.

10. Finish neck edge with a narrow rolled edge that has been cut on the bias from collar fabric. Hand sew a loop and button at back of neck edge.

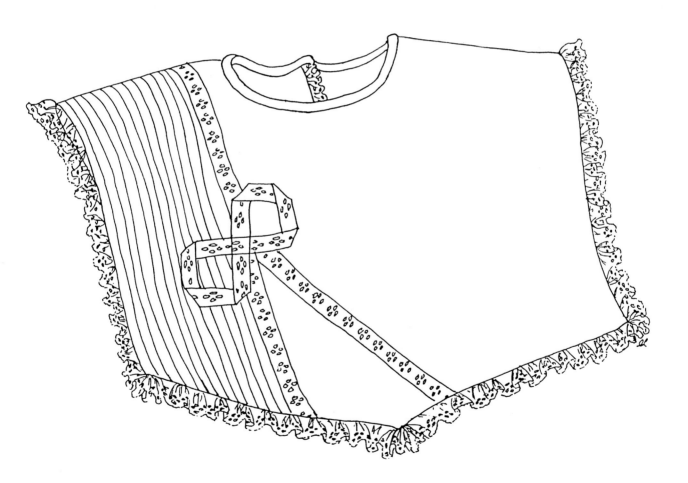

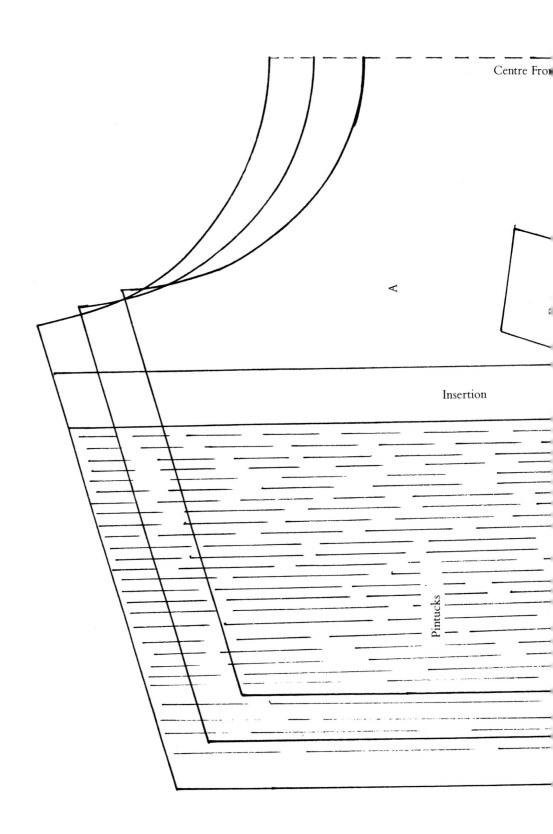

Centre Front

A

Insertion

Pintucks

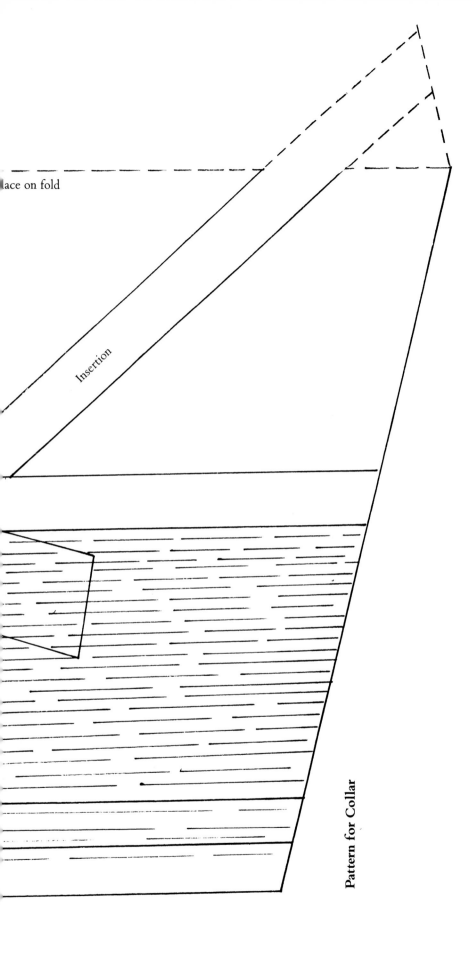

Place on fold

Insertion

Pattern for Collar

Large

Medium

Back

Small

53

Large

Medium

Small

Back

Pintucks

ECHNIQUES

MITRED CORNER

When mitring lace or Swiss edging, measure carefully down to the corner, turn the trimming at right angles, ready to go along the next side. As you do this you will find there is a surplus of trimming at the corner. Pin this carefully to get a straight mitre, then stitch with a fine zig zag from the heading of the lace towards the edge. Do not stitch through the edge (Fig. 25). With a Swiss embroidery, zig zag towards the edge and straight through it (Fig. 26).

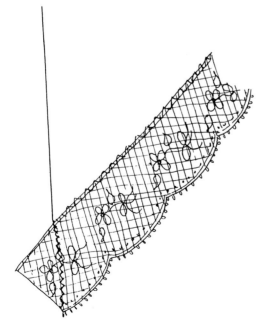

Fig. 25

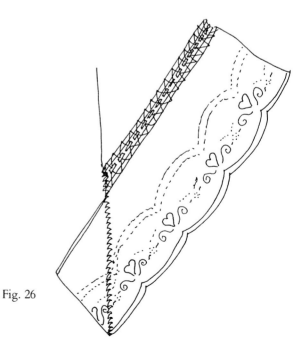

Fig. 26

PROJECT 7 – TRAIN SUIT

TRAIN SUIT

MATERIALS
Batiste
Swiss edging: 64048
Entredeux: 30054
Buttons: 24883

Using the shirt pattern provided and the techniques you have mastered, along with your basic dressmaking skills, cut out and assemble the shirt.

The sleeves are cut from the Swiss edging and the trim around the collar is the same edging cut down to the desired width. The pants are a basic boy's pattern for button-fastened shorts.

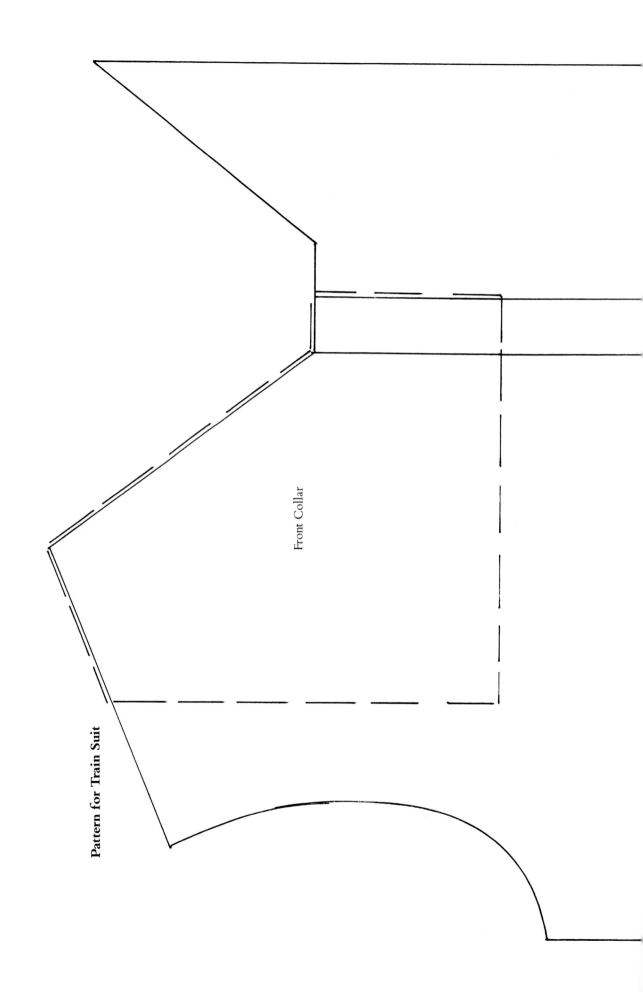

Front Collar

Pattern for Train Suit

57

Centre Front

Cut 2

Front

Fold

Collar Back

½ cm (¼") seams

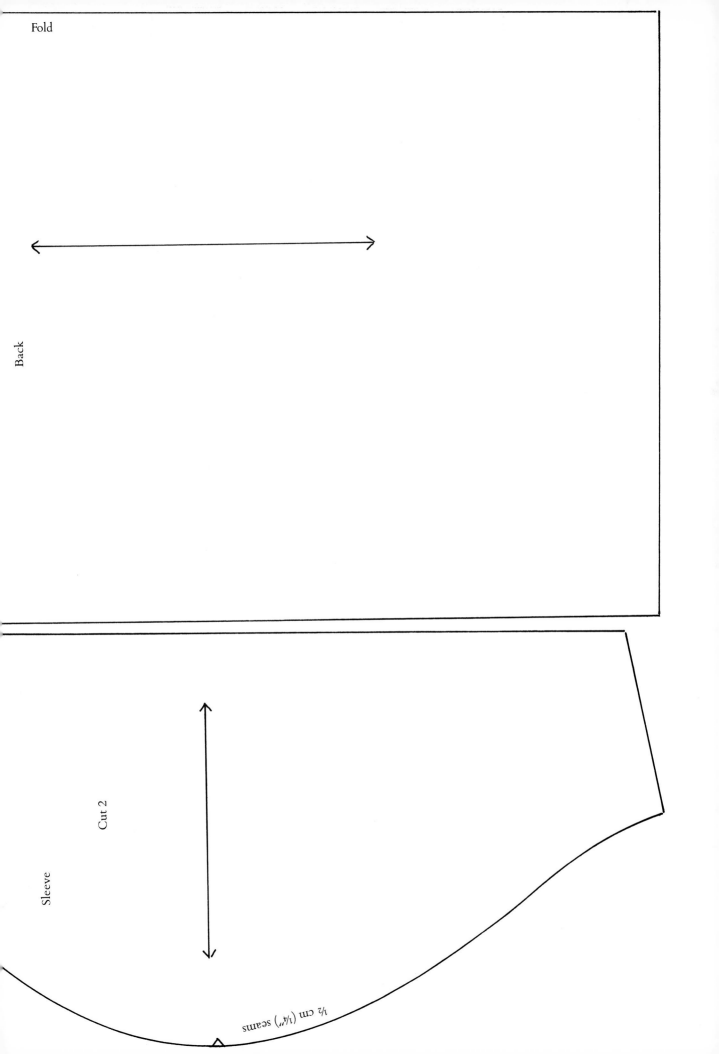

PROJECT 8
– BLOUSE

BLOUSE

MATERIALS
Batiste
Lace insertion: 1332
Entredeux beading: 61925

A basic blouse pattern has been used to show how you can change designs to suit yourself.

First, make some sketches showing where you would like insertions, pintucks, etc. and also what shape you would like this to take. Make up your piece of 'fabric' to suit your sketch. Place pattern on top (as in Lace Collar project), cut out and make up using basic dressmaking techniques.

The blouse may be finished with some pinstitching on the machine or some hand embroidery.

PROJECT 9 – BABY'S SHAWL

BABY'S SHAWL

MATERIALS
Wool challis
Wide lace edging: E7913
Narrow lace edging: E7912
Ribbon: 2mm (¹/₁₆″)

A square has been used for this shawl. Roll and whip all around the edge; the corners may be rounded if you wish. Measure around the shawl. The length of the wide lace edging will be 1½ times this measurement.

Gather the edging, measure and tack in position on edge of shawl, making sure you have enough fullness for the corners. Join the lace. Place the ribbon on top of the heading of the lace and, using a wing needle and a stitch on your machine that looks like this ☐☐☐☐☐ (no 166 Pfaff 1475 CD), attach the ribbon.

There are many ideas you can choose for the centre of the shawl. I chose an oval with a bouquet. A sketch of the bouquet is included in this book for your use. You may photocopy it to enlarge or make smaller as you wish. Using the same idea with the ribbon as the edging, stitch gathered narrow lace edging and ribbon, following the shape of the oval. Embroider as you wish.

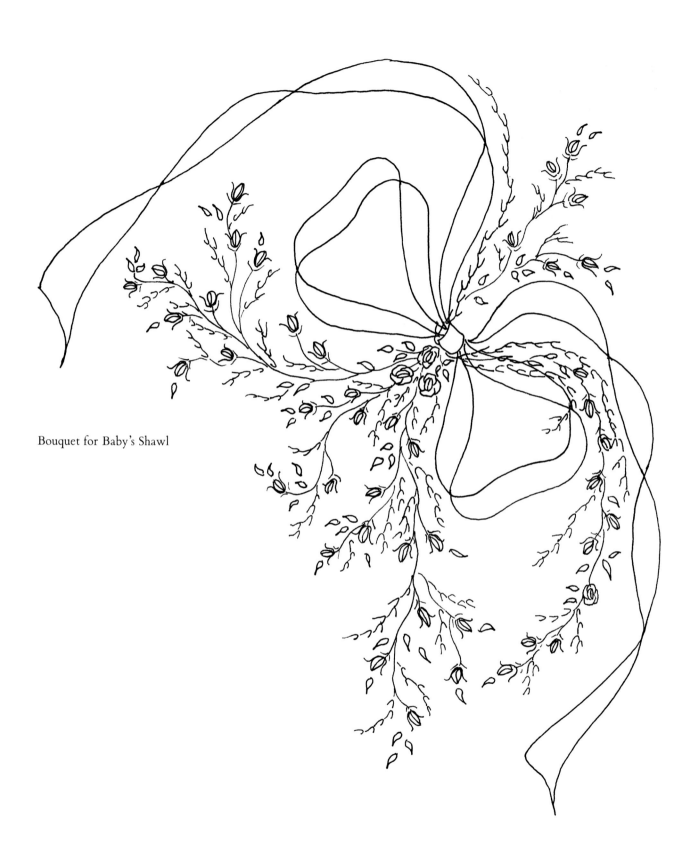

Bouquet for Baby's Shawl

SUPPLIERS

For your nearest stockist of French Val laces, Swiss embroideries, fabrics and patterns, please contact:

Needlecraft International Pty Ltd
96 Rowe Street
Eastwood NSW 2122
Phone: (02) 858 2815

Wholesale enquiries welcome.